BUBBLE
KNEE
AND OTHER POEMS

BY FRANCESCA FOXCROFT

ILLUSTRATED BY KATY FOXCROFT AND ELLIE PERRY

C000047530

First published in 2021 by FoxBooks Publishing in the UK.

Copyright, Francesca Foxcroft, 2021

Francesca Foxcroft asserts the moral right to be identified as the author of this work.

Paperback ISBN number: 978-1-8383495-0-9

Ebook ISBN number: 978-1-8383495-1-6

A percentage of the proceeds from the book sales are to be divided equally between POTSUK and YoungMinds.

Edited by Kim Carr.
Book cover design by Rob Williams
Book cover illustration by Ellie Perry
Illustrations by Katy Foxcroft

In support of

YOUNGMiNDS

To Kit, who is forever in my heart.

ACKNOWLEDGMENTS

Firstly I wish to thank my supportive and beautiful family,
Oliver, Katy and Max.
And to all my wonderful friends and family who have
encouraged me to write. I love you all.

Also thank you so much to Ellie for doing the stunning
front cover design.
And to my beautiful and talented mother, Katy, who
brought my poems to life with her brilliant illustrations.

INTRODUCTION

I began writing these poems just under a year ago, initially as a kind of therapeutic way to let all my emotions spill out onto paper. I had always enjoyed putting pen to paper, unloading all of my stresses and worries, and also recording the joyful moments that I wanted to remember forever.

Soon I had a large collection of poems in my notes app, and I decided to begin to share them with my great friend Ramsey (whose poems are much better than mine will ever be). He inspired and encouraged me to write more, and here we are.

I decided I wanted to share my collection in the hope that someone reading it may find some comfort or solace in my silly words, in the same way I do when reading poetry myself.

The inspiration for the poems has come from all areas of my life, but also other's lives and therefore there are some poems that have not come from my own experiences, but from my empathy for those around me.

These poems are authentic in their honesty, in the way they are not trying to be anything that they're not. So I hope you, reading this, enjoy them in their eclectic and genuine state.

THE
POEMS

BUBBLES ON MY KNEECAPS

Kisses from my mother as she washes my hair
her love is felt through every touch
my arms do not work and the soap gets in my eyes
I watch the sun set and my gratitude is bursting

I think of a time when I could do things myself
little by little this becomes the norm
forming my new life and mind
my peace is calmed by the bubbles on my kneecaps

SHINING

It makes my heart beat a little slower
Makes my skin a little warmer
My eyes a little wider

It makes my smile a little softer
Makes my brain a little faster
And makes my peace a little calmer.

FOREVER

I stopped saying forever
When I realised forever
Wasn't limitless

When you can't fathom an end,
They come in fast and wide
They come, even after what feels like always

Forever laughs in my face
As even within itself,
the very word is fleeting

We love people
Whether for a minute, a moment or a lifetime
Perhaps without this word, deceit wouldn't win

The time stamp that spoils all
Perfect words and imperfect people
Because even within infinite hours, there is an end.

FEELING ALIVE CAN BE TRICKY

Feeling alive can be tricky
Especially as life can be sticky
but feed yourself with
love
and
hope
And maybe that'll help you cope.

THE LUMP IN YOUR THROAT

We fight and we scream but you're who I like to be with
when I'm sad
because your warm blanket of love swallows me up until I
can't think.
You may think you're bad but I know the truth
and I still love you even when you make me mad.

Your stupid hair makes me smile
and that crazy laugh that rings in my ear for a while
You think you lack worth and yet all I see is growth
You're worth every sleep-deprived night
and every cuddle to clear the lump in your throat.

I'm sure there'll be years more tears for me and you,
but I wanted to say this because well—it's true.
You excite my bones and fill me with fear
but somehow I can't help but feel calm when you're near.
The only thing I know is the love that we share
and God am I scared that it'll one day not be there.

Somehow your head is not always pressed against mine,
and it seems that sometimes we're fighting against time.
You told me you'd hold me until I fell asleep.
I know that you meant it because it's my heart you still
keep.
I love our friendship and I love your big heart.
I even love you, despite your ridiculous smelling farts.

This poem could go on and on, as I could talk about you all
day.
I know you're bored already but push on and I'll pray
that you find some sort of comfort in my words as I do with
yours.
Even if you are talking about planes or cricket scores.

I know you think you let me down,
and I know I let you think that.
The truth is that I simply treasure our moments
even if you're across the phone for a chat.
Whether it's dancing Living La Vida Loca at the Hancock
or watching movies until we fall asleep
I'll always be here if you ever need to talk.

I'm sorry you can't steal my cigs anymore
but I've heard you've learnt to roll.
You're talented at everything, including making me whole.

SITTING DUCKS

Close your eyes and imagine a lake
Your very own Nirvana where the sun shines
and the world is sitting patiently at your fingertips

It's waiting for you to grab it with both hands
and embrace these beautiful people
beautiful places
things that seem incomprehensible are right there
in front of you
like sitting ducks.

MY THOUGHTS, MY FEELINGS

I stare at the letters in my mind
as they swirl together and confine
my thoughts, my feelings

GENTLE HEARTS

Be gentle always
as people hide the wounds
that bleed the most

So shower people in kindness
It works like medicine,
curing wounds ferociously

TIME TRACKS

Shut out all the windows
we're not looking for love
we don't need anything more
than ending up on my floor

Doing nothing with you
feels like jelly and ice cream
loosing track of time
between our sweaty dreams

LOST

Passing by a little fountain
my thoughts go to and fro
Time begins to blur
new sleep the moon's pale glow

There's elegance in being lost
I forget what I may want to hold on to
those silly today's and tomorrow's
that would usually drag me down as rain begins to lag

The rhythm briefly slows
As I breath in and out
inhale—exhale—they say
and it'll turn your life
about

Peaceful and benevolent
a gift from our moonlit
God
The fragrance of rain upon
the grass
says don't be afraid

Let's dig our toes in the
wet sand
and let the cool waves
wash over us
alone hand in hand
just me
and you.

Try to stay calm and grounded
As it'll help you from feeling surrounded
I think of a still lake of peace

and dreams on a floating leaf

Darling we lay in silence
and there's no whirring of thoughts
We think of nothing and yet are content
this is the way I am fulfilled

Cry if you need to, as
crying is a beautiful thing
Let your emotions fall down
and surrender themselves to you

IMPERFECT

I wish to describe every inch of your face
your quaint freckles unsymmetrically placed

Your gaze is deep with brown eyes that crease
when joy bubbles up and you laugh from underneath

Skin like the moon; cold and white like Christmas
my fingers memorise your pale palate of soft kisses

Unruly blonde hair, refusing to be tamed
framing your freckles, they are one in the same

A hint of a scar on your upper right cheek
Hopelessly I watch you, my eyes become weak

As I fall into a slumber, I go over every detail
Every perfect imperfection I follow intensely like brail

Finally I land on the most prefect pair of lips
they intoxicate my body with every single sip

Gently you pull me deep into your space
I will always remember your kiss, your love and your face

TINNITUS

Why does this tinnitus of technology drive me to such
extremes?
Why does the buzz of my phone make my heart skip like
I'm some sort of machine?
Why am I the only one who doesn't look the way I should?
Why would someone love this one, surely they'd have
someone better if they could?

CONSUMPTION COMPULSION

I touch my skin and try not to scream.
It screams at me, as I itch away
through your tight seams.

The pressure is vast and beauty is set.
How can these expectations ever be met,
by me: tainted femininity?

This virtual decree has
each hair, each mark, each flaw locked up.
We learn too quickly, and receive runner-up.

Breathe in, look neat
and don't you dare eat

Consumption compulsion drives me to *you*

Your hazy days make me feel full.
Addictively disgusting,
the smoke in my lungs pulls me through.

Shameful hunger plays with my softness.
your fumes keep me going
until it's bone and a smile.

You are sickly but I like the
smog.
It's somehow euphoric.
Feeling full, yet empty, but
now catatonic.

NEVER THINK

Broken strings
now they're all twisted
all I see
is smoke

Close to you,
bitter safe
I will wrap you in my arms

Something about having that
deep dark love
that no one can grasp
or see into the depths of the eyes
like we can

It's heavenly
But we're in hell
caught in a web of lust
you pull on one string I'll pull the other
we fucked each other
as we fucked each other up

Bound by love now
never think
what's in your heart?
what's in my mind?
do we even understand?

SCARS ON YOUR SOUL

My love,
I could cry at the sight of you.
You hold so much sadness in your eyes,
as you stare at me with distance.

Darling,
Where are your thoughts,
as I know they lie not with me?
Tell me your worries and perhaps I can help.

Sweetheart,
Open your heart
and you will see that I care.
Who are we together, if we do not share?

WHISPER

I could feel his lies brush across my skin
like a whisper of thick black smog
that clogs
my very existence.

MERRY MEMORIES

We gather round, all glowing with Christmas cheer.
Happy memories of singing and laughing,
so lucky to have all our loved ones near.

Smiling, sharing and so much love too
As we gazed up at the star lit sky
It was then that we knew . . .

No matter where we wonder, no matter where we roam,
We will always have each other
to bring our hearts back home.

9TH AUGUST 2002

She's divine in the way she fills my life with light
and she fights fiercely for my happiness without any
expectation
sunsets and vino, she is my heart and my family

When I think of her, I think of health and love
I think of the way her beauty is delicate, and her infinite
generosity can shut out your problems with a blink of her
bright August eyes

We are symmetrical
and I miss her when she's gone
I think of her roaring laugh and I replay our memories
of snuggles and smoking

She makes me feel warm
No walls, no flaws, no forced smiles
winding down my heart is torn

Do I love her more today, or tomorrow?

REST

Rest
Liebling,
Rest
Rest your weary head on my chest.

And I promise I will never move again.

HOW?

How could I not have fallen in love with you?
I knew you existed. That was enough.
But now,
I simply look for you in everyone.

LEMON DRIZZLE

Sleeping is luxury
and a deep sleep is a gift
when my eyes are blurred and I'm feeling sick
I punch a hole in the wall with my fist

My silk sheets are warm
and my dogs breathing is comforting
but why won't my dreams of health
truly take form?

Tears fall as my frustration grows stronger
that fist in the wall becomes my vision
my heart is anxious
and I can't hear the serenity any longer

The pain is there
oh yes I can feel, hear, see and smell it
the ultimate puppet master
that doesn't care if life isn't fair

Pain doesn't treat you with respect
even if you deserve it
It doesn't know when to stop because you just can't take it
any longer
It has no limits but my body does

My legs are now floating
and my breath is still
my heart has stopped pumping
and Jesus is there with his lemon drizzle coating

MARSHMALLOW MIND

I'm trying hard to concentrate
yet my mind is stumbling over your words
they come like arrows
two and then another
unrelenting
unlike you at all

There was a time of peace
when butterflies flew
and kisses too
your smile is still reflecting mine
yet now we both know the truth

The dimples in your face make my heart beam
you're soft like a marshmallow, but you're sickly like the
rest
you look at me with pity but how can I expect anything
less?
Our sparring is therapeutic for you and that marshmallow
mind

You're fighting with yourself
your irritation with me can only be set free
by you
let go and I'll keep you safe
and lend you my love completely

CHAPPED LIPS

I miss the way liquorice stuck to his lips
and his grin would grimace through his smiles and tears
endless red with endless fascination
into his curious neglected mind
with which he pondered so

I miss the years of time where we relaxed in the certainty
of definitely
and I had never thought of years of yearning grief
or the woe inside his eyes of blood
his heart was still blossoming, still beating
even with its cracked veins filled with fickle love

Nothing more could be said than this—

Too much woe had chased after another
one life was taken.
Breathless—
he breathes in my thoughts
he loves in my daylight dreams of paper planes
his smoky memories are lit like lanterns
floating high up in the sky where you know he's laughing
now.

He carried me.

I'll write to you soon, and relight the red
so just hold on tight to that piece of my heart
and let your heavy eyes close with a yawn of peace.

TEARS

Your voice turns dark
and I can see your lips go red
you look away from my eyes
your gaze low, your body slumped on the bed

I think of others
and how their emotions fall
you are softer yet tearful streams
flow most of all

You hold your breath
suppressing these feelings
eyes sore with the sorrow
as we dwell on life's dealings

You deserve so much more
I hate to see you sob
eternally my arms are open
healing your wounds I take proudly as my job

Softly brushing your hand with my lips
our fingers intertwined
deep and fast my thoughts wonder
will you ever be mine?

LAUGH

His laugh is in his eyes
As he slips into relaxed joy
it comes from within
like a child with a new toy

Immeasurable warmth
spreads through me when I hear it
echoing through my heart
his face completely lit

Absorbed in his giggles
I fall fast and hard
transporting me from my troubles
he pulls down my guard

BEDTIME STORIES

My favourite bedtime story
is the discussion between my lips and yours

CONDITIONAL LOVE

Whose love is utterly unconditional?

Endings drive their way in
unexpectedly soon
for far too many.

Their secrets now with you,
and yours with them.
But you are strangers each day and night.

Together you feel free,
the love feels so much bigger than anything
anyone has ever experienced.

And yet September comes around again,
with nothing but separation and distanced distain.

So I ask once more . . .
Whose love is utterly unconditional?

A GIRL IN LOVE

Can there be anything more perfect
than a girl in love?
As she skips through her world,
like an angel from above.

Nothing is unhinged,
Nothing too hard to handle.
It's a joy that can last forever,
never stubbed out like a candle.

Hope is all around,
and the air smells like him.
Who knows what the day has in store?

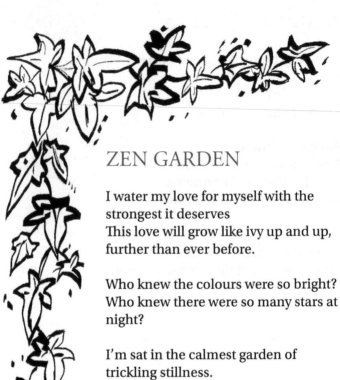

ZEN GARDEN

I water my love for myself with the
strongest it deserves
This love will grow like ivy up and up,
further than ever before.

Who knew the colours were so bright?
Who knew there were so many stars at
night?

I'm sat in the calmest garden of
trickling stillness.
Leaves sway in the wind
my mind is quiet, completely
motionless.

QUEBEC

I've never been to Quebec,
and I've heard that I should
It's filled with people who are only good

People who see joy and
people who accept your past
People who are still, even when life seems too fast

I crave this Quebec style of life,
and this zen-like state of mind
Learn one thing from this poem: choose to be kind

TURNING

Is this the spring that I've been yearning?
A long awaited symphony of May
brightens my brain from baffled sleep

The sky turns pink
with delighted glee
as I step out from underneath the shaded tree

A little step today
forever indebted to this little life
of May

FALLING

Nobody can ever truly capture
those feelings of euphoria
from when you've fallen
hard and fast

Fallen in love that is.

We don't say rising into love
Because really the idea of
The fall captures it the best:

To fall in love
is to fall into complete blind and stupid vulnerability.

And I love you
Blindly and stupidly . . .

THE GREAT PAIN

Today I fight a little harder than usual
My bones feel like they're rotting
my veins are writhing in pain
I can feel my blood scream in undeserved strain

Pain is a funny thing I think
each person is suffering differently
beautifully decorated in the heroism of fighting yet
everyone thinks they're hurting the most

PILLOWS

As I lay here thinking about this life
I surround myself in pillows
Enveloping myself in comfortable blankets
Protecting my body from the night.

As the world around me spirals
I know I am safe
I am safe

THE VARIATIONS

So many different versions of my day that could play out
Only God knows what's in store.
I trust in his power, his work and his love.

BEAUTY DOESN'T CEASE

Just because it ends
doesn't mean the beauty of it ceases to exist

When flowers droop their heads
we don't regret buying them

We accept that there will always be an expectation
of an expiration.

But nothing beautiful could ever be a waste.

SHE CRIES

My mother's eyes are red with opaque agony
Black makeup smudged across her rare face

How can I help you?

IN A BOTTLE

Oh how I wish I could have captured your presence
and kept it in a bottle, for times like this.

TO YOU

My love
To you
I am sorry
I took up too much space than I deserved.

ROCK BOTTOM

One day
when all has come crumbling
and you've reached that bottomless pain
the place they call rock bottom.

Somewhere down there
you will stumble across your strengths
and soon enough
you will stand again
even taller than before.

UNTANGLED

A constant buzz.
This mind of August chaos scratches like a bitch
from the inside out.

How can I find a silent moment inside myself?
There are no white walls in my mind.

The lights flicker as another thought pushes its way up.
I suppress it, once again.
And again.
And again.
Only to have it reappear a moment later.

Somehow people find a small dose of calmness
by sitting still—no even stiller.
But I can't seem to let go.
Not yet. No.

Ricocheting anxieties zig zag through my judgement.
And there are no breaks here. No intermission.

How do I untangle these words, peoples and patterns?
Please teach me to rock my anxiety to sleep.

SMILING THROUGH MY SIGHS

I can't think of what to say
But I miss your thick voice
I wish you could hear me
But I know I gave you no choice

Now you must think
I am some sort of child
You know you mustn't use me
But somehow you're beguiled

Our eyes are too wide,
And too red for this heat
And yet when you kiss me
I fall at your feet

There's nothing particularly special
But still I want more
I think my love for you
Goes right down to my core

God I miss you and your chatter
Even though I roll my eyes
I look back on old photographs
Smiling through my sighs

SNOW

He was like snow
cold
frosty
but you couldn't help but smile when he smiled,
and he melted on my warm impact.

EYES SHUT

Shut tight my dreams follow the sky
clouds of grey and hoards of eyes
on me and this thing that is my vessel of life
this thing he took from my feminine skin

Thief I would say
I would scream if I could
He took, he stole the things he knew that he could
Shut were my eyes and hers and mine
But not those eyes which we thought were only kind

Tennis balls of tears trickled down like treacle
thick with disgust and all the things one cannot wash out
stained with dirt as he cut with his rusty blade
yet his facade of wealth never to fade

Fade not my life on this now treacherous path
trekking through this torturous syrup,
that sticks like love does.

But time does not work you see,
as no amount of time will allow me to flee
from the grasp that he has on my tainted body

LETTING GO

As I notice how easily the petals drift down from their
flower
I am envious of their effortless separation

They let go.

I watch and wonder—
How do they just let go?

PREPARED

Is there anything that could have prepared me for this?
Should I have been ready?
Was this inevitable?

Blindly shaken by a piece of thread
which I clung onto frantically
screaming for help
for anyone.

Silence.

Stumbling, falling, now covered,
surrounded by this shroud of discomfort.
A discomfort I would feel forever.

Drained of hope, desolate sobs of dirt snuck out
as I struggled to keep my tears silent
not wanting to be found—again.

My fists closed so tight I could feel my sweat
trapped inside them
I couldn't breathe.

I cried until no more tears would come
but the shame lasts a lifetime
and that feeling of losing control.

Fire burned in my cheeks
as I heard what I knew was Hell
I silenced my wounds, clutching my tainted body.

I prayed that I would drown in my own tears
as an emptiness was left in my heart,
I knew he was here in the room.

Red hot tears silently streamed
carving a crevice in my tender cheek
as he stood there in rage.

I can still smell the sweat
long after my tears have dried.
Is this what I am left with?

The shaking does not stop,
into the night I feel the sting,
of the devil that took so much.

Should I have been prepared?

MY SCARF JUST A LITTLE TOO TIGHT

How can anyone ever see the things that bother me so?
Your soft touch is like a burning rod of fire on my skin
It viciously drags me back to that place of—

You may not see it and yet I am screaming inside, driven
back to the white of my skin and then there's his face
that has taken too long to forget
And yet your unknowing hand on my shoulder
etches every detail
just as the scars on my emotions are marked forever

My uncovered body is always jealous of your surrounded
skin,
as it's protected by your clothes
Bare bones are like torture as the icy water glides fiercely
over my shape
Perhaps it's the vulnerability of being unclothed
that chases me down to the depths of my memories
and drags them up over and over

Things so tiny that haul me back to July
Even if my scarf is pulled just a little too tight
only the slightest difference sends me swirling into
unsteadiness
I cling to the sides of my mind and clench my fists
my whole body follows
Not relieved until I am safely in the arms of my dreams

WINDOW

I stare through the window
to unexpectedly see your face—
Pupils dilate.
Heart races.
Throat closes.

ARE YOU ANGRY?

"Are you angry?"

At you?
Never.

AS THE RAIN POURS DOWN

As the rain pours down,
I hear your voice echo through my heart strings
across the phone your euphonious laugh
makes my day seem bright.

As the clouds turn grey,
the stories of your adventurous day
turn the seasons into summer
and my heart glows with golden sunshine.

FLOATING

Do you ever feel so high
you stop to catch your breath
to look down
and you see
everything that you've achieved—

Suddenly
It's like you're floating.

MY DEEP DOWN SILENCE

Somewhere down there
in the depths of my existence
is a perfect stillness
that echoes silence.

One day it will reach the surface.

ESCAPE HE SAID

Romance: pure animal passion
The way his body drove itself into mine.
My love, pinned down by his
Fierce grasp.

When we fought
We fought like lions
Attacking my neck, he protected my heart
Ripping down my walls

My arms above my head
There was fire and more fire
Maybe it was our broken souls
Stuck together like a jigsaw

He took my breath
Saving me from my dreams
My worries
'Escape' he said

Our rhythm was uncomfortable
Unconventionally beautiful
But then we would love and fill in the pain with
More fire

I'm out of the cold
My sins burnt my way out
But my only direction was to him
The desire sent him down into me

Uncontrollable fire
As *you* look through my rose glass
my arms are set free
and I can't lean on him any longer

This much desire
Would kill us
But together we're lions
Losing my way through in his grey eyes

Full of lies, my lips
Touched his lips
Desire driven by our bodies
Intertwined into one

Two blushing roses
Ready to stand
Too tender to seal a kiss
And it goes like circles

APOLOGIES

There are so many people
so many things
that I am deeply sorry for.

Regret is a dangerous thing
but surely everyone ponders on
the what ifs?

What if I hadn't let you down?
What if I hadn't come round?

Realistically
I can't go back
but if I could
I would just say this:

I am sorry.

FORGET

When you're not there
people forget about your face
they neglect your space
they forget the promises they made

CONNECTED

When you're sad I can feel it in my heart,
I can't tell you the pain I feel when you cry.
Your tears sting my mind like a bee

THEY'RE JUST PEOPLE

We put people on these pedestals.
We think that they're perfect,
but that's not fair to them,
or to ourselves.
Nobody could ever, or will ever live up to the expectation
projection.

WHAT'S DONE IS DONE

You can contemplate on the past as much as you need to
But in the end we all know the truth . . .

No amount of thinking or overthinking could ever change
what has happened

Regrets ring true and they ring loud
Some may have many, some just one

They haunt you
and there will never be a way to shed their baron
memories of remorse
And so . . .

Move on.
But most of all,
Forgive yourself.

RELIEF

I stare and I stare at the photos on my wall
And I wonder if it's true at all
Maybe they were joking . . .

I held your soft face in my hands
and stroked your stubble too.
You're perfect to me, I just hope that night meant
something to you.

You told me that you loved me.
Can I hold on to that forever?
Should I?

I CAN'T FIND THE WORDS

I'm so sorry
I just can't find the words
How could I ever begin to imagine your loss?
The fragile bandages round your courage can only hold so
long until
they whittle away, soaked with eerie tears.
I write and write but I'm tongue tied.
Thousands of words bounce left and right
but I can't put them together,
to employ the empathy I feel.

COTTON WOOL

I hate to hear the sounds of his tears
as they stream, they scream down his flower face.

They don't deserve to use up his emotions
nor does anyone who can't see his irreplaceable
compassion.

As I hear his deep sighs of agony
I wish to wrap him in cotton wool to keep him safe.

He is the one who shares my genes,
So lucky am I to call him my best friend

Our laughter echoes through the millions of memories
He and I will never be apart

OUR LITTLE LOVE

I know that it was real
but it seems so long ago now
that I question our sincerity

I cherish our little love
forever and a day
definitely was our always

SOULS

My soul deserves peace
and so I choose to forgive you.
Not because you're sorry for the pain,
but because my world is better without the burden of this
grudge.

VACANT

And your lonely mind
floods my life once again,
now that you've exhausted all your distractions.

You're still vacant in your speech
and your touch, as ever, painfully cold
but how can I turn you away?

Do we continue on this merry-go-round
knowing that we're wasting time?
Or do we be brave . . .

I know you by heart
and when we're apart I'm missing half of me
but does that mean forever?

Just because you're here
I hold on tight
maybe once you leave my lines will become right.

I hope they do.

WALKING AWAY

That day
when I walked away
It was like saying every goodbye I have ever said—all at
once.

FAILURE

I've always assumed I would do something great
but the way you look at me . . .
like I'm nothing

I'm entertaining the prospect of failure
and pushing the pebbles back out to sea

Maybe I'll fall at the last hurdle
or perhaps before I even get going

Maybe it's not even about floundering
but about the plain stillness of my life

ARE YOU SCARED?

Do you walk down the street knowing you're in danger?
Always on the look out from an attack from a stranger.

Do you close your eyes at night and remember him in your dreams?
No matter how much you want to forget it, you can always hear the screams.

Do you overthink your clothing, knowing who might be staring?
Or do you walk right out the door, not even caring?

75

STORMY

His storms of love
are dangerous when there's deception
Who dared to cause suffering to his precious youth?

He will riot for their contentment,
wishing for life to grant their wishes,
so he leads the heartache in other directions.

Saddles are for the sufferer
and yet he holds no troubles too tightly:
a guarded defence of family glue.

So do not underestimate the things he will do for love.
Connected forever are those
who earn this fix.

START AGAIN

I wish we could float away
fly up to the surface and just start again.
Slowly bring it down,
room temperature is all I can take for now

Let's just watch our troubles fall like autumn leaves
and let ourselves fall deeper and deeper—
Is that enough?

THE SAME

Isn't it strange
there is someone thinking the exact same thing
right
this
second.

THE TRUTH ABOUT AFTER

No one ever talks about after.
The long and tedious process of
Falling out of love

There's no doubt that there's pain.
Just as you and I are the same,
both foolishly waiting

You would think some kind of relief,
would spread across my smug face
Finally, after all this wasted time

Tears and tears have I shed . . .

And yet somehow I am saddened?
My heart is no longer heavy but perhaps
that was the only reminder of what we had

These laughable words flow and yet they are not
any less true:
I miss missing you?

I loved loving you. And now it's gone.
I'm free but I feel lost.
At least before I had some sort of pitiful purpose

Now I suppose I must trudge on
And no doubt will fall again
But know that I feel the space of where you once were

Even if it was so long ago.

PRECIOUS PETAL

Selling love is her danger
Lust is her treasure
Driven pressure is her flaw

Weary eyed fucking
With strangers that rot
Inside her wings

Crumbling, screaming inside
this angel needs something:
It's vital to find her way through bronze dreams

Young and sinking in the crowd
her petals fall
crumple and shatter, as do her dreams

Wet fingers over her fearful mouth
not a sound
just that of pain and pleasure

Wings of wisdom beyond her years
Wings of frail love
Wings off and she curls up trembling

TRICK ME

Trick me
and prick me with your sharp words.
I'm drowning in your reflection
but you can't even see your own direction

You gloat your wealth,
of frescos and kinship
Yet your torture is clear, despite all your efforts.
It's your eyes full of troubles that I'm scared of

Down the path you lead me
until I retreat back into myself
leaving only you
and your outstretched fingers

Your lines are like thistles
yet there is love here, I can see it
The green of your eyes, is overgrown with
your neglected past

It's raining salt
masking your tears
You swig on that reliable thing
She is your friend you say?

The stench of your breath says otherwise.
Slumped in on yourself, that's when I see it
Crimson, almost black
It relentlessly runs

Blood on blood

You look up and I see through your soul
That sweet nod that showed
you're just a child, willing me to stay

Your eyes that triumphed
Are now closed with regret
Your face is unmistakably stained by your mistakes,
that carry you away

And I see your outstretched fingers.

HEART TORN IN TWO

What to do
when your heart's torn in two?

Someone you love
has been taken up above.

Breathless and gone
it's too hard to move on.

Mourning is a mountain
your tears like a fountain.

Climb higher each day
but down, there's only one way.

Drenched in sorrow
"It'll be better tomorrow".

But it's not remotely close
My whole body is morose.

What to do
when your heart's torn in two?

Cry a little more
But feel their love to your core.

Pray to the Lord
and trust in his accord.

Angel in heaven—

I love you.

CHAMPAGNE

Love feels like
champagne bubbles in my veins.

HONESTY AND HONEY

Because of her, it's always light in my world.
Even in the darkest velvet night,
the inky sky is perfectly black

Our friendship grows in our souls,
and shines through our eyes,
into our hilarious memories

The push and pull of
the instinctive vines
that burst with health and sweet sweet dew

I am well schooled in love
but this love is built in our bones
and nurtured in our secrets

I am content because she is there to protect me
and save me from any harm that befalls
no matter what; this is my sister

If she is crestfallen, I'll wipe her gloomy tears
and laugh until the sun comes up
dancing our show over and over.

There is nothing like vulnerability to establish
love that acts like glue, and grows never repetitive
so sweet like honey, our cosy days are my favourite

Even halfway across the world,
I could feel her love.
This is forever.

I DO NOT LOVE YOU

I do not love you because you're a shiny gold box filled
with precious jewels and gems
I do not love you because you're one of my oldest friends
I do not love you because you're flawlessly perfect
I do not love you because you're polite and have respect

I love you because you're jagged and ripped
I love you because you're aggressively gripped
I love you because your darkness shines through
I love you because you're unapologetically you

I TOOK JESUS TO BED

I took Jesus to bed
and let him roam around in my head
places and things
brought me no shame
but when He found people
especially his name
blood rushed and gathered at
the apple of my cheek
innocence fell away
eroded by the memories I tried not to keep
blushing pilgrims
kisses flew from room to room
I insist we weren't children
and were already fully bloomed
But He cast my pursuit aside,
took a deep breath and sighed
the same slutty stories
that I once boasted
quickly became the fire with which
Jesus roasted
and snubbed out my femininity.

WHERE DO YOU GO?

Where are you now, as I lay awake and think of you?
Where do you go?
To see you, I turn. To know you, I yearn.

LIKE YOU'RE IN LOVE.

Why must you kiss me like that?
Like you're in love?

LOSE YOURSELF

Go out and look up at the big, tall trees
and the shadows on the floor from the soothing breeze
Memorise the shapes that the clouds make in the sky
Better yet, sit and stare at the stars that fly
The flowers grow and the sun shines bright
Listen to the wind as it calls your name at night
Now that you've seen such incredible things through those
eyes
How could you ever live an ordinary life?
Protect this world and don't let it stumble
This beauty is essential if we don't want it to crumble.

WHY CAN'T I WRITE?

I read and I learn about how to string a sentence
and I suppose I could do that quite easily.
But really I can't write like the others can
I can't put words together, and make it sounds like fresh
flowers
My words are concrete, heavy and rough.
Why can't I write like them?

UNLIKE OTHERS

Unlike others, I welcome the rain
It soothes my thoughts and relives my pain.

Unlike others, my mind is instantly relaxed
the pitter patter on my window is my afternoon romance.

It's dreary but it's cosy, and I enjoy the warmth of my fire
juxtaposed by the storm we watch as we retire.

A PENNY FOR YOUR THOUGHTS

Today I will give you
my final pennies
A penny for your thoughts
and your love forever

Today I will tell you what my plans hinge upon
and how, they are hung aloft the sky
but I will always give you
my last penny

Soft snow upon the grass lies in unrest
listening to the sweet swoon of our penny wishes
in wells that splash back
not wanting to abide

Our secrets are awake, even now
our pennies are stolen and sickly
because our thoughts are not our own
no ablution stands ready to catch our bitterness

But my love
I will always give you my pennies and my pounds
for your thoughts are priceless
I wish to capture each one and wish your wishes true

HOME

I'm not as exciting
as the other girls you invite here
I'm not as gripping
as the stories that they tell,
while I'm sipping
on tea
they sip on vodka with a twist
and spew up all the drama,
that I've surely missed

I'm not into any electronic music
and no doubt if you catch me I'll have Paulo on repeat
I don't do drugs nor do I want to anymore
my head is buried in books
and chocolate is my vice

I'm not going to be the devil on your shoulder
and of course I'll always be here as your steady bolster
I'm not a high speed chase
I am a Sunday afternoon
I can't tell you lies, not even when you want me to

but I am a home
and I am yours when you need me

AIRPLANE

As I sit here and say my final prayers for today
I look out the window and stare at the dark in the hope of
some relief
Glancing up, I see a plane as it blissfully glides away
to a place of quiet calm, where worries float from view
I close my eyes and imagine this place, and wish that I too
was on that plane.

WITHOUT PRIDE

Do you know anyone who lives without their pride
who loves without their stride
and who clumsily gives their all with humility and effort?

MORNING COMES BURSTING

It comes in warm and bright on my weary eyes
The sun swings round my room with enough energy
to drag me out from under my cosy dreams.

FLAMED

His life was imminently flammable,
the school bell on the tip of his tongue,
itching to hear that sound of liberation.
Fire tore him apart,
red hot fingers that pulled each part of his life
underground, where flames bite.
As he willed the bars of his cage to melt,
his unconscious mind sparked ideas
of choking on hot ash.
Burning as the hot ribbons of light
cascaded down his beautiful lies.
A phoenix cries,
igniting a fire, undeserving
of attention.
No matter how much the passion
runs rings around his softness,
even as the red seeps its way into his veins,
he never let the fire touch her

MY ADDICTION

I use my breath to steady my thoughts
and I can no longer find them in my mind's eye
they are silent
and although they will return as soon as I'm done
for a moment, there is peace and serenity
like a tidy room

I'm addicted to this introspective reflective.

THE SOFTEST KISSES

Eyes that could turn your soul inside out
and read every secret you hold on tightly to.

Lips that would tease my heart
and kill me with the softest kisses.

You were my home and you were my war.

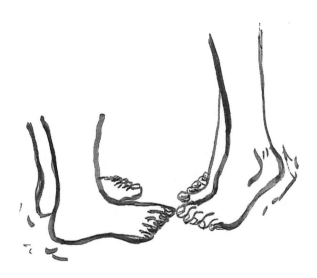

A REOCCURRING DREAM

The pain that burned like fire has faded
into an icy numbness
scenes of ashy black
the edges of my mind filled with memories
I can hear my lonely heartbeat begin to slow

Ragged shallow gasps of air
minutes pass and I'm still lying there
People swarm but I can't hear their voices
trying to save my little life
how childish their endeavour seems to be

My fragile heart beats one last time.

UNMISTAKABLE TOUCH

To describe the perfect kiss
would be to describe your lips

Your touch is unmistakable
as my body ignites

I can feel your passion
and your love through your grip on my waist

In my heart,
we are always kissing

OUR SECRETS

Your eyes bore into mine
with that crazed look beautifully sculpted for me
Biting your pride, as you turn to walk away—

I follow
slammed against your ambitions
that served you so well but made me bleed as second best

How can love do these things?
I'm out of my own head
but instead you're inside

Hands round my neck, my power is taken
as our justification echoes through the plain halls
but you always made sure you held me close

Calling my name
I am pinned with your weight
You tease me with the tip of our secrets

MAYBE ONE DAY

I'll be wondering down the winding road of August
and our eyes will meet with unique crimes.
We will be fully healed, done all the inner work that has
come before,
and ready for our time.
There will be no filter, no expectation, living contently in
any weather.
Giddy hope of anticipation, we stare and we lock into each
other's heartbeat.
Pulling me into the kiss that stopped all anxious thoughts
in their tracks, I would know
that this was a dangerous hand.
Delving into this breath of a windowless box.
Eternity with gates wide open.

Maybe one day.

HE COULD

Have you ever felt darkness?
Of course you have.

But have you ever been
fully consumed by such a darkness
that you couldn't fathom a way out?

Well, he has.
This ocean that he faces
every
single
day
runs deeper than you and I could ever know.

Yet he continuously
finds the strength to pull himself onto the shore,
no matter how sharp the rocks are that he's greeted with.

He lets go of the comfort and
that familiar salty sensation of drowning
that he knows so well.

He carries me
and helps others find their heaven
whilst his mind fights the biggest feud with himself.

He is strong,
and takes the part of him that is broken
and makes it a ghost for one more day.

Being strong isn't being free of fear.
It's laughing in the face of anxiety,
and putting yourself first when everything seems so
wrong.

He reaches deeper to find even more strength to hold himself up.
One battle after another.
And when he can't any longer, we will be there to repay his kindness.

GAMES

Do we still play these games of children
or have we risen in our love that we do not need to
anymore?
I feel saddened and hurt but really who am I to know
what's right?
and what's wrong—
My empathy is lost in your dream world tears
as their fickle trickle runs rings around us all.

FIGHT

You must fight your own wars to save yourself
or else you'll be forever floundering through this tightrope
life.

TAKE ME BACK

Sometimes little scents of Spain
or our song
take me back to that summer
In love.

As the sun sets on our perfect day and the rays disappear
we await the silver moon and its stars
and watch the trees shadows create new pictures on the
candle lit table.

Amid the perfume of summer bloom
we play the games of the evening, smiles across our sun-
warmed faces
The music of laughter echoes through the mountains that
hold us there together.

Our cozy little cottage captured our fights and our
emotions
as we lay snug in our bed of white lilies
whispering tender streams of consciousness with no
judgement

Day in and day out we watched your silly films
and listened to each other like we never have before
and it was enough to just say I love you.

Each day opened like a love letter
and the warm words of light radiated onto our welcoming
skin
and just for a while our fairytale was so beautiful.

And yet of course
summer turns to autumn and our passion fizzled

and my shaking body was once again crushed by your
impulsiveness

Of course life isn't a story you get to make up
but everything happens for a reason.

IN YOUR ARMS

In your arms my storms quell,
and I finally find some peace.
In your arms I am home,
and my worries begin to cease.

IF YOU'RE IN LOVE

If you're in love
listen to this
because I know that you're thinking about
that person and their kiss

If you're in love
surrender to your feelings
I promise this is real
you're not simply dreaming

If you're in love
hold onto their heart with both hands
and never lose your grip
even if it means you can't stand

If you're in love
know that you will argue and
you will fight
but you must work through
it all
and your love will fly high
like a kite

THE SKY AT NIGHT

When we look at the sky at night
how far back can we see?
Can we see yesterday and last week
or are we looking at last century?

Stimulating stars are disrupting my sleep
and yet I have little care for astronomy
perhaps I'm beginning to grow weak
because we don't waltz at all nor play hide and seek

Time and clocks and chiming too
misreading all the signs that the sky leads
and it's unusual for my letter to get lost in the post
but you knew exactly how to press all my keys

A young lady who drowned in little flowers and
champagne
was toying with her prey, plenty of noise to cover her
tracks
but of course her time was up
and they heard her scream as the knife went in her back

I watched, aquiver with anticipation
ready for that happy ending that is so ingrained in my
brain
but it's good to change with the times
and supposedly we need to stay sane

I jumped through hoops and your payback was real
and all for what?
just so you could intimidate my nights
and finally convince me to feel?

HUNGRY HEARTS

Tucked away where we both
were too comfortable for our own sanity
Laughing uncontrollably, silliness with no bounds
We are toddlers giggling at everything and nothing
has ever or will ever be this funny

Clinging onto each other for stability
My rose-tinted glasses show nothing but smiles
But deep down my scars are written in your handwriting
Memories I keep to hear the sound of your voice
when I miss your deep love and breath on my cheek

How could we pour so much of ourselves into each other?
And be left with hearts shattered and scattered round
these Andalusian hills that hide our secrets and our flaws
Eyes lock you were controlling my body, my mind and my
heart

The hazy heat hides not only our laughs but also
the screams
At night I sleep with my back to the sound of your dreams,
waiting for those morning eyes of regret.

I'm sorry.

How can someone's love control another's actions?
Surely there are limits and no one would let me get in this
deep. But no.
Who knew anyone could feel this passion?
How twisted our trust became.

This Golden prison, that we return to each year, thinking
we can escape unscathed.
I was enthralled by his very being.

Under what I think he put me in—a spell of affection,
unbreakable.
My heart was hungry.
Hungry for his acceptance.
My legs wrapped round his waist tighter than his arms
were ever around me.

THE DAGGER

Passing him the dagger
he traced the tears down her face, with his eyes
filled with fear and temptation
to drive the dagger straight through her heart
of course
blood stained trust
skin, once paper white, was now lost
red walked its way down the hallways of her heart
but she was happy
for he liked her crimson blood
he wielded her like the same dagger that
he wounded her with
icy tears on her sleeves
oh how she loved to make him smile
even for just a while of
bloody love

ENCHANTÉ

You enchant me with your eyes
and delight me with you accent
as it sounds like sex.
Expensive cologne that vivaciously kindles my senses
and your mysterious eyes that let on just enough
for me to be hypnotised by your suave movement
round this city of romance.
Your presence is like a smooth jazz song
that plays effortlessly round and round
making me dizzy with excitement.

WRITING

I think once and for all
my world is falling
around me

I tried going back to the source
but I am even more lost than before
even further away from what I want

I wish I could go back to when
things were simple
and my body could do the things I wanted it to

No limits to what I could do
or what I wanted to achieve and yet
my goals are still the same but just now out of my reach

It's tricky not to dwell on these restraints
and pity my desperation
but I know I need to try and try and try

And so I sleep and I imagine that my life was the way it was
I dream of my aspirations of writing
And so I scribble down these poems in the hope of fire

THE SKY IS WEEPING

I look up and little drops sink into my skin
I breath deeper and smell the warm summer rain
It's a moment for my soul to connect to a deep sense of joy

Although the sky is weeping
my head is happy and songs sing bright in my elated mind
and for a short while I embrace the cold as a gift

READ

I love to dive into a new novel that promises new lively
thrills
Or even joyous peace that brings a smile to my face and
my heart
You never know what brilliant lesson you may learn
or gains you can bring into your own life

A love for turning the page
and discovering a whole world past your own
I want to feel connections and my fingers to linger on
each word, poised and ready to discover more in the next
chapter

THERE WAS YOU

Somewhere in between each breath
in the midst of March
or every second Sunday

There was you
there was you
there was you

28

As I walk unsteady round and past the eager eyes
I see your face and my heart stops.

Every touch is my surrender into your life
because you build me up and make my lines
stronger and bolder
always a more fierce way to tackle each battle
and fight this time just a little harder

You make me believe in August
and its story telling quality
being able to tame the mind of blushing shyness

COME FORTH

Enter into your passion
and don't let go until you've accomplished everything
you are willing and you will do this for yourself
Who can stop an inspired creation?
Come forth and buy into yourself; to believe in your own
capable words is to truly see your future
and work for it.

MY TWISTED VALENTINE

Comfort is never key when it comes to February
and everyone is desperately searching for an antidote for
loneliness
Solitude feels like failure on this day of love
and so we yearn each year for a kiss that lasts just a night
Some validation that we are not the problem
Curiously scanning the room, staring intensely at those
who eat their oysters with intent
Eyes meet with a smell of danger
and we fall into this twisted valentine with ease
only to be left the next morning, and we are once more
alienated

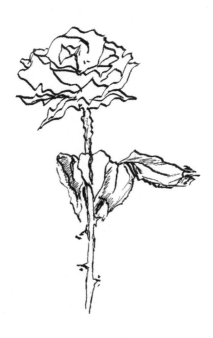

COMPLIQUÉ

Our inexplicable love started as
the most simple melody
and at the heart of it was you

You add to me the depth and richness base notes
suspiciously full of tears but truth be known
also full of content moments of heads over our heels

But of course it could never be that simple
compliqué is my specialty
Soon our melody became a symphony of chaos

CASHMERE

Who knew love could be so exquisitely romantic?
full of blooming roses both red and pink
and exotic orchids that bloom with our connection

Your touch is like cashmere
perfectly blended for my embrace
which of course I do, over and over

VAN GOGH

Such beautiful swirls of blue and yellow
that evoke such pain in my mind
as I ponder on your meaning and your thoughts

You envisioned a life
of love and stars and starry nights
that would touch every eye and every heart for decades

Paint of Amsterdam shows up in my life
wherever I look and so we return back to this song
that sounds like you

You were alone, you were alone
An asylum of obligation
You, the crazy genius, enjoyed your tranquil insanity

Tonight I sleep under the stars, and listen
Don McLean and I are watching and watching
as your disintegration plays out in the cruel constellations

This was your view
and now it is mine
How much must we cry
until our tears are seen?

Your masterpiece of the
sky is where I hold my
peace
And I must thank you
eternally for that
as I thought my
nightmares would never
cease

UNMEMORABLE

My face seems to be unmemorable
as people come and go
forgetting night after night
my name.

SUNDAY

Sunny days and Sunday
the home stretch of the week
belinis and buck's fizz
smoked salmon on the side
of cheers and laughter

A game of chess
and a plethora of clues
from the crossword that swings
right round the room
because Sunday is for smiles
And roast potatoes too

Pyjamas all day
duvets and black and white movies
that remind us of a time before ourselves
but the sound of the fire brings us back
to slippers and Sunday songs

A grizzly walk in the rain
to blow the cobwebs away
The touch of a hand
to remind them everything's okay
and there's nothing quite like a Sunday

POWDERED LOVE

I paddle in your shallow love
beautiful and heartbreaking in equal measure
soft just like yourself and candle lit dinners
powdered snow balls
that sting our red raw fingers

INTOXICATING

Your bright blue eyes cast a spell that first magic night
A fairytale of New York, and the phantom between our lips
As we ran through Times Square

It doesn't sound like real life and yet somehow you are
Your captivating gaze of promise
that make me fall blissfully into your grasp
and somehow you fell just as quick, slotting into my life

Tension through the falling leaves of golden red and
brown
in my foreign clothes and coats of fur
you wrap me up warm as we kiss on the ice
Thin ice?

You know I left a part of me in that city
With the blinding intensity of neon lights
and deafening noises of afternoon traffic
There's an imprint of your fingertips on my palm

Hardly knowing anything about you
How did I fall for your Manhattan honesty?
The way your eyes bore into my gentleness
like no other, admiring and obsessing—
I feel loved

AFFAIR

What comes first, the perfect love
or the Affair?

Exciting deceit brings bubbles of flavour
that I can revisit again and again
but as the passion comes flooding back

My guilt is tenfold

SOFT SNORES THAT I KICKED

We lay like lovers
and revelled in our comfort
completely cozy with kisses of calm

How did we ever get so lucky
to find our matching piece
that fits like a lock and key?

Soon we drift
and time passes quicker than I'd like
as every minute with you is precious

Suddenly I'm awake as your arms close around me
like my own personal blanket
made of tender solace

You lay serenely, still deep in your slumber
your soft snores that kept me awake
I kicked to make them cease—

But now I want them back.

VANILLA

Am I really this tedious?
Utterly dull and miserable in this pain?
My Lord, am I allowed to live such a monotonous life?
Or will I die before I grow old?
I am sick of this repetitive sickness that kick and kicks
and of course does not know when to stop kicking.
It has no regard for my mind or body.
But I know my spirit is strong, strong enough to fight sigh
after sigh
But is my body?

I have not always been this vanilla I promise.
I used to be fun with no concern for blood work or heart
rate
And so perhaps I will just have to adapt . . .
Adapt to show my life through colours on my clothes

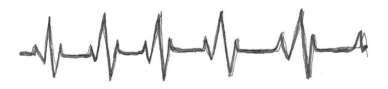

I CANNOT STOP

Somehow when life halts
I take control by writing
I write and write
and I cannot stop

I cannot do the things you do
but I can write more than you

And so I write and I write
because there is no limit on my mind

This is the thing that my sickness cannot take away
It is mine and only mine

AMBITION

Grand gestures of theatres and roses
make me swoon for the miracles you could give
But the only love affair that I hope for
is the one between you and your ambition.

Your drive inspires my moves
and your achievements move my life further forward each
and every time.

HIGH ON YOU

I'm somehow under the influence of you
and your traditions that you have created
I'm high on your life
and the way you spend your day
I'm lost in your world
so I can't help but stay

YOU WIN

"You win"

But my darling
We're on the same side.

THIS ONE PERFECT THING

I feel like I'm dreaming and I'm about to wake up
so please take my lips again so I can stay here a minute
more
In the morning I will be blurry
so please let's indulge in our velvet night
This one perfect thing
that I don't want to lose

KISS HER

Kiss her
kiss her slowly, take your time, like there's no place you'd
rather be
Kiss her like you're not waiting for something else
Like you've forgotten any other lips, with curious childish
delight
Inhale her sighs, and laugh in sync
Kiss her stupid
kiss her silent
kiss her until she forgets how to count

HEART'S NEEDS

Your heart is a vast and tender thing
You cannot continue to try to shrink it into what someone
else can give it
You cannot pour all your love into a vessel that cannot
contain it
You cannot give all your heart to someone who's heart is
closed off
You cannot love someone into their potential

So walk away . . .

A THOUSAND BROKEN HEARTS

Those who are near
let you fold away like a feather forever
Goodbye is like a blanket of stars
and you said goodbye to a thousand broken hearts

Hold on tight to the pictures in the frames
because you were always the one to hold us
I remember loving you
and I know you felt it too

It's your birthday and we are all still here
A thousand broken hearts
as you are in a shroud of peace
I'll remember forever the way that you grinned

BENIGN

Is your soul benign
or do you inspect it like you're mad?
Or do you lie in the quiet
knowing you're simply just sad?

He knew there was no way
and yet there always is you see
Clouds change, but as do we
Colours too as they sweep across our sanity

Perhaps they didn't listen because they knew too
that deep down their souls are twisted through
Lovers shout but they are benign
How could we ever have known the signs?

FRESH

A walk ago now
I remember strolling around and through
picking berries here and there
I stopped to breathe

I stopped because my heart was racing
and my lungs needed their drink
Deep breaths

Into my body I took in the fresh air
and felt immediately alive
Its crisp cold edge hit my senses like a sugar rush

This air was invigorating
and I felt my strength return for a while
I stopped again to breath

Soon I felt like I was floating
this medicine that fiercely rejuvenated my spirit
is something I am forever grateful for

OLD SOULS

Maybe,
just maybe . . .
We knew each other before
in our first, second or third,
lives are measured in numbers
Perhaps it's a case of when we were meant to meet
and when was our time

This was not our time
but we are old souls you and I
old conversations that run like clockwork
A spell of Just and Us

REFLECTING

Your tears reflect in my happy blue
but for some reason it's never just me and you

I wish that everyone could see all our smiles
but you are covered in sticky tears that refuse to cry

Your eyes are bright as they wait patiently
they watch willingly with compassion, I can't forget how
they look at me

Games that I despise, and I know you do too
it's complicated enough, don't involve her too

In the air I will feel your feather from here and now
a tangible forever with sugar and vows

Please prove that none of these illusions were in vain
it was all for us and our August rain

It's okay if it rains
it's okay if you need time away from dizzy pains

your thoughts of love
your thoughts of planes and getting away
your thoughts of cigarettes and the nearest ash tray

I will love you in whichever
colour
size
language
font
way
that you wish

MOVE

I wish we could swap
we could swap
and turn our voices into rain
or another place

I wish we could interchange
and just like that
someone else would love the way I do
and hurt the same

They'd carry my past lighter than I can
because to live is to die
and really I'm just trying to fly
So let's try?

I'll tell myself this lie just to stop the cries
of August that I just want gone
Why couldn't I have been September?
Sessions end and I go back to my old patterns

So why can't we swap?
You'd take this weight—
wouldn't you?

A STRANGE CRY

Today I am tired
and my head is heavier than yesterday
I'm in a sleepy storm that flits between night and day
And I can't find the right door out

Each door is heavier than the last
and I'm beginning to lose the hopeful flare
that keeps me from fleeing.
Today I am tired

I think of my cells and their tendency to hibernate
they ridicule my every reason for existence
Why must they admit defeat when I am still fighting?
Abandoned by my most loyal defence, I am lost

Suddenly I let out a strange cry
and my delirious delivery into each day reminds me
of my imminent mortality
But that's enough for today

THE VOICE IN THE WIND

Sometimes when I let my imagination run wild
I hear your voice in the wind

It takes me completely off guard when
I hear your voice in the wind

I can't quite believe my ears and my scars burn when
I hear your voice in the wind

It's husky and it's rich enough to make my heart churn as
I hear your voice in the wind

Too much has happened now for you to be really here, but still—
I hear your voice in the wind

OBSESSION

I think
I think about love too much—
But really who defines what is too much or in fact too
little?
Must I attempt to trap my thoughts and not let them fly?
I'm dwelling and accidentally indict my past
Without knowing I slip into a solemn solo and listen to
them cry

SUGAR

I'm feeling like sugar recently
finally energised and sweet
like a candy cane keeping me up into the early hours
as I tap away on my keyboard

Finally there is a spring in my step
and as I venture into the world I had forgotten
I can feel the sunlight reaching down to my sleeping cells
to lift them higher and higher out of their impossible
cocoon

As I stroll down the road with my new spirit
there are the places I thought had been lost
that I dream into fruition every day
I enjoy having the energy to miss them

For now, I relish in this sugar
knowing its fickle nature
but I embrace the vitality that has blessed my day
and the strength I feel keeps me going—

SEASONAL

Sometimes we hold grudges against particular months or
seasons
when life hasn't gone to plan and we are left melancholy
For you it may be Winter, as the sky's light fades out faster
than we were prepared for
It's easy to slide into a cycle of sorrow
But this year is a new leaf

Life is far too short to hold onto such anger
and associate a particular time with any sadness
especially when there is so much room for joy and love
So do not dwell on last year's cold nights
and focus on making this one as warm as you can

SCARED

I'm scared of what I don't know
I'm scared to get too close
I need a lesson in letting you go
so please
please
please take me out of my comfort zone

WHEN WE MET

When we met
I had no idea how important you would be to me

I had no idea that your sweet inviting smile would
turn into such a rock, such an imperative part of my life

You melted my jealous bones into forgiving love
and somehow bring such joy into everything you do

Pain changes people
some become sour and some silent

But never had I realised that it could bring great change
until I met you and your eager silver linings

HYDE PARK

We lie silently on the boney earth floor
as the dry summer grass welcomed our visit
This was a goodbye that I had never wanted
but knew you needed
A goodbye that would not last long
yet painful all the same.

We stared deeply into each other
completely consumed by your face
the world around us passed by, in slow motion
Our little Hyde Park corner
where we threw grapes and kisses flew too
Forgetting our plans of returning soon

The sun beamed onto your summer gaze and
for a moment
it felt like heaven
You sucked on pomegranate seeds, and my hair blew in
the breeze
such childish dreams of aisles and silly things
And yet . . .

Soon came that goodbye that I had hated from the start
As it grew ever closer, your eyes would turn away
too good at the painful word you throw my way
But you held me in Hyde Park
our little corner forever
I will remember these days and the way you kissed me that
summer

EVENING ROUTINE

I sit here and watch you go about your routine
teeth brushed, your hair is next
Intently staring into your own gaze
the mirror offers you no love and so you turn to me

Toothpaste-stained lips
you are perfect in your evening hygge
and yet you won't be content
Perhaps if you could see through my eyes

I never craved attention
until I tasted yours
Now that I have
I'm forever wondering when my next sip will be

POSSIBILITIES

These impossible branches of possibilities and paths are
as frightening as the unknown
because really they are unknown
and ambiguity in this world is strangely agonising

It's like a tree of errors and paths of the right way
and of course, left
Each decision has falls and roses and so who is it to decide
which is best?
If I hadn't done that, who knows what may have
happened . . .

And so . . .
When I think about how different my life may be if I had
stayed alert
and not assumed my safety
I am immediately taken away from myself
out of my body and into a no man's land that I can never
escape

FORGET ME NOT

She's my crisis call and my cosy sleep
she's the one who always makes sure that I eat

She's outgoing and strong yet vulnerable with those who
are lucky
She's as crazy as a loon but sweet like honey

Ups and downs, but through it all
she'll be there to pick me up when I fall

STRANGER FROM THE PAST

I've forgotten how to write about you
stranger from the past
your lips your eyes I'm trying to find
your voice I let slip my mind

and yet
you are so bitter
and can't pretend to know why . . .
I was just thinking of how much we have grown
but perhaps it would have been better if I had just left you
alone

Why must you think I am to blame?
When in truth you're the one who came
to me
to me you came with all your pride and spat it out
like a dummy that she made you suck on

Don't you dare blame me for your insanity
when I put your mind back together
piece by piece
A jigsaw that I never intended on starting
A puzzle that demanded never to be solved
And the pieces scattered round my life as I frantically
search for the missing piece

Of course it was lost
and you knew it was too
Forget my pity and you can forget my love
erase it from your memory
and let our years drown thereof

MY SKIN

His words are fine wine,
but always spoken by a man.
Healing medicine for us girls who
take shelter from the storm.
His pen is sharper than his sword,
his words bite and don't let us go,
like an infant's favourite chew toy.
He grins his sins,
knowingly snapping our necks repeatedly.
But never ceasing to lick his own wounds,
as if no one has even had thoughts of such a woe.
He smiles as St Valentine cries
Yes, he laughs in the face of love
but pretends to have answers for my heart
break, snapped right down the middle of
this European road.
He bows his own name into every single bed,
imbedded in my skin.
Proudly taking his place as the hero of the hour.
So sour his lips taste,
flavoured with his half-truths.
His words may be fine wine
but I'm going to decline...
this time.

THE LITTLE THINGS

It's always the things that seem insignificant
that I cherish and I relish in
I run upstairs, fingers frozen in the frost
the burning shower water runs over my skin
and time felt at peace with stillness within

When the sun starts to rise
and it finds your eyes
you yawn with excitement for your day ahead
a new opportunity for becoming the person
you wish to be in your head

Waking up to the smell of pastries
on a tray with a single flower
breakfast in bed and a precious duvet love
and kisses between the crunch of marmalade toast
pyjamas and pinky promises

Childhood innocence that comes with a smile
from a stranger passing by
happiness growing from ear to ear
like how a spring flower opens
A show of dimple joy

Driving hastily from one place to people
too fast to notice the sun setting perfectly
and then suddenly on the radio
the sweetest sound
your favourite song echoes
around
patience is instilled and instantly
you feel at ease

I THINK

I think I am broken
the words are getting stuck in my throat
I think about your stubbornness
and all the things you wrote

I LISTEN

I listen to you talk
and watch each fold in your lips form new heights of
excitement
my interest peaks at the way you move
and how your eyes catch fire in a conversation of politics
you notice me and my pyjamas or the way my eyes roll
back as I pretend my annoyance

DRIVING

Driving down the country dandelions
I was 17 and you
were golden
sitting next to me

FEEL THE SUN

Close your eyes and feel the sun
warm and orange beneath your eyelids

MOST OF ALL

Most of all,
Laugh
laugh so much it makes your stomach ache
or until you can't laugh any more
Let all your childhood smiles fall out into your world
Laughter is like the summer rain and a songbird too
A cloudy veil lifted and we can finally see with some peace
These honest rumblings of the soul bring our memories
alive

Open your arms your hearts and your mind to the people
who bring you joy
the people who make you feel safe and whole
Give back to them and show your heart
Pick up the slack when days are tough
and never give up on those who value your spirit and your
space.

INDEX

171

Postural Orthostatic Tachycardia Syndrome (PoTS) is a type of autonomic dysfunction, characterised by an abnormal increase in heart rate that occurs after sitting up or standing and causes severe, unrelenting symptoms such as nausea, dizziness, fainting and exhaustion. It is a serious condition that can significantly affect the quality of life, and also can cause other autonomic dysfunction secondary conditions. There is currently no cure for the condition, but POTSUK is an amazing charity, providing support and continuing research to try to find a cure. A percentage of proceeds from the book will be going to the charity, and hopefully this will raise awareness as there is little known about it, even amongst doctors. The average diagnostic delay experienced by POTS patients is six years, and so I have been incredibly lucky to get my diagnosis in under a year. And yet the disease is not a rare one - 1 in 100 teenagers develops POTS, and twenty-five percent of patients are so disabled they cannot attend work or school.

If you want to read more about PoTS and Autonomic dysfunction or donate money, please (any of your spare pennies pleeeease) head to www.potsuk.org.

ABOUT THE AUTHOR

Miss Francesca Foxcroft, born and raised in North Yorkshire, at the age of 19 shares her incredible talent for all to read. She has found time whilst studying English Literature at Newcastle University, to write beautiful words which will make you laugh, cry and give comfort. What started as a cathartic release of her thoughts has transformed into a beautiful collection of poetry, exploring topics of growing importance, which go unmentioned and must not. In her first compilation of captivating poetry, she has created something which allows us to explore the angst of teenage life. It has moments of darkness and fear which grip us, times of silliness and love which bring us warmth, as well as lust and passion, to blush the cheek. The collection has been randomly placed within the book to express the way in which her thoughts came to paper. Its aim is to emotionally spin you around at the turn of each page. Her words resonate, allowing us all to know that in times of "blue" we are never alone. The poet's bubbly and compassionate nature shines through her artwork along with her vulnerability, perseverance and strength. Accompanying the poems, are a collection of evocative sketches and illustrations, to encourage the reader's imaginations.